TABLE OF CONTENTS

FATHER VOIDS OR "HIM ROIDS" MEANINGS

According to the definition, the meaning of Father Voids is empty, heartbroken, resentful, living with or without a father, known or unknown.

1) Some reasons for fatherlessness are divorcing and out-of-wedlock births. There is data that supports the way fatherlessness affects society. It makes children more likely to be poor. Fatherlessness makes them more likely to be a drug or alcohol abuser, drop out of school, and suffer from health and emotional problems. Boys are more likely to become engaged in crime. Nevertheless, girls are more likely to become pregnant as teens.
2) Fathers need to be just as attached to their infants as mothers are. When both parents are involved with the child, the chances of growing up emotionally healthy are greater.
3) Fathers who are not physically present may still have a confident presence in the life of a child. Nowadays, people are in many relationships more efficiently than ever. Even though a child may not have their biological father in their home, they can still have consistent engagement through social media, FaceTime, etc. This engagement from a distance can keep the relationship positive until they can meet in

person comfortably. There are few excuses for not being there for your kid.

4) Father Voids mean lack of spirit, love, acceptance, missing momentum, and psychological harm to growing up. Those effects can present throughout a child's life. Having a missing father, you are on the verge of being an orphan. That is when you have lost two parents. The absence of a father can be a traumatic event. Having no known father is almost the same as having no father. In our modern world, solutions always exist. Many father voids occur due to accidents or on purpose. Nevertheless, they can be filled.
5) It is said that children need at least 21 years of love from both parents as they grow and mature into adulthood to be emotionally stable adults.

"Him Roids" means just like the word Hemorrhoids. The only difference is "Him Roids" is a spiritual, emotional, and mental pain. In comparison, hemorrhoids are physical pain from a medical issue. The treatment is that they both need some kind of relief. One may need therapy or medicine. The other may need family, forgiveness, or communication to work things out or time spent together in love and kindness. If it is Him Roids, we suffer with them. It is best not to sit on it but get up and do something to improve things.

MY VOID

FATHER VOIDS

I knew deep down in my heart that I had something missing. I felt that my mother's boyfriend was a part of our family since I was a child. I thought of him as my father. I went along with believing it. It was because I had nothing else to believe except overhearing as a child a word or two from others talking about it. However, later, I realize that he was not my biological father.

The first words I heard were from my mother's brother-in-law, named uncle Tyler. He said about Charles Wiley, whom I knew as my father, "He is not your father." That made me very angry because I had nothing else to believe. It did plant a seed in me because it just might be so. I could see what he meant. When he said, "that is not your father" to me once with anger, my aunt replied to him also with anger, "shut up, Tyler." At this time, I was about nine years old. No one had mentioned my biological father. I started to figure it out when I questioned my mother about my name. That was when we were talking about the social security check that came in the mail. It showed my last name on the check as Lucas Jr. My mother's boyfriend's last name was Wiley. Children are intelligent, even though they do not talk like that sometimes.

I heard the word the second time from my cousin Karen. She wrote a letter to my father as she told me about it. She was 13 or 14, and I was about 9 or 10. She wrote me a letter as well. She said certain things to me with my mother's permission. I got a little excited to hear back from him, as she did. The love of my cousin gave me this opportunity to have a little communication. Eventually, I met my father for the first time since I was six months old. I visited my father for one week. However, I was supposed to stay two weeks. My father was doing the same thing, due to which my mother left him. Yes, he was actively addicted till then. Even though he was there with us during the visit, he was not there spiritually. One morning my father tried to sit me down and speak to me.

Nevertheless, I could not do it for some reason. I had no interest in what he wanted to say to me. So I popped up off the couch and ran outside through a side door to play with some rocks. He said to my mother out loud, June. She answered he was just like you. My father said a few words to me as I played with rocks, "there are spiders out their watch out." I replied to him, saying okay.

I started to figure out why my mom did not want to bring up my biological father. After my visit, I realized it was not a great experience after I finally got to see him. The problem with my mother's relationship with him was because of his active addiction. He asked everyone he introduced me to for money on my visit. He told them he would repay them when he got his check. I remember it felt a little uncomfortable. It was in the way of my visit and getting to know him. After I came home, my hope of having a good healthy relationship with my father sort of diminished. He passed away a year after I visited him. So what little hope I had for a relationship was then lost, I thought.

I acted out some in my life, not knowing that my father's void was a part of it. I rebelled against my step-father because he had become an alcoholic. He had a tense relationship with my mother. They got married in 1967 when I was 9. Then they got divorced in 1972 or 73 when I was 14 or 15. Another father void was created by the divorce of my mother and step-father.

Later I became a father and started out well. Nevertheless, after a while, I had the same experience as my biological father, active addiction. The progression of addiction was a downhill journey. The only cure for some ways was to quit wholly or entirely surrendering. In 1994 my life changed. I was able to be a better father. I understood more of what my father went through and why my mother protected me from an active addict. Now, I see this as love. I forgave my fathers. Then I started to adopt the attitude to be a good father to my children. So, I started to think of the father I would like to have. I succeeded in being a good father to my children. However, It was possible only because I was in recovery and not in active addiction. God, the father, became the greatest love in my life. I stayed open to God's love through my experience. People on my journey had shown me my love. My experiences of love were helpful. Much, at first sight, my voids might not resemble love until the sharing and attention took place.

Even if one is not a father, nonspiritual forgiveness can affect their attitude toward other fathers. It may hurt their relationships with many men; brothers, grandfathers, uncles, cousins, friends.

Today I realize that without my forgiving attitude, my fatherly attitude of wanting to be a good dad would not happen as it did.

I went to my father's grave to pray, to see where he was at Portsmouth, VA. I placed a cross on his grave. I kept reminding myself of the words my mother said that were suitable for him. It was that he had done well when he read his Bible.

I sought out to find my sister.

I changed direction when I could not find her. I started to look for any of my father's family. The first find was Sandy, and what a bonus!

During my search, the people, the documents, and the DNA replaced my void with sharing and caring. It was simply loving.

My void started to fill when I met Sandy Lucas. I never thought how powerful the impact of this person would be on my search and the finding of my family. It all started when I used the telephone book to search last names in Florence, SC, from where my father's family was. I found a

David Lucas. It had been just like the name on my father's paperwork saying his father. I called and got David Lucas Jr.. He tried to help me but said this was the wrong person. He told me someone else to call, but no one seemed to know about my father or heard of him. I felt at a loss and a dead end. I kept sending letters to ask for information from Lucas' in the phone book in Florence. There was one response from a lady David Lucas sister in law. However, she did not know my father or his family.

One year later, I started my search again. Nevertheless, for some reason, I went right back to the same phone number as David Lucas. This time I had more information than before. So I called, and David Lucas Sr's wife answered. She had no answers. She thought it would be helpful if her daughter Sandy Lucas called me back. When she called, her first question was whether I was a white man or not. I replied no. She then said that she was going to try and helped you. Eventually, she did. Through Sandy, I met Pearl, Mrs. Brown, Ruby Bass, and many of her relatives. A few of them had some knowledge of my father, which was golden to my spirit. Everything that was said about my father was considered a depot in my void. Good or bad because I was open to it.

DEPOSITED: LOVE

Sandy introduced me to Pearl first because she said she met my father when she was five years old. I got Pearl's phone number and called her. She answered with a sweet voice. I asked her if she ever met my father. She said yes. She said she lived in the home of Sandy's father, David Lucas. She was about five when she met my dad. He came over with Sandy's father, David Lucas. Their mention of my father being with Sandy's father caused me to have hope that I was related to Sandy's family. This was a solid deposit into my spirit. I would then call Pearl every few days to hear her voice and hoped to remember something else. I would be excited sometimes to call Pearl from work to hear about anything. Her life, South Carolina life, etc. After talking to her for a few more weeks, I talked to Sandy had found someone else. I told Pearl that if I visited South Carolina, I would look forward to meeting her.

Sandy had found a very elderly lady named Mrs. Brown. Mrs. Brown said she knew of my father and grandmother named Eva Bass. I got excited again and opened to whatever they could tell me. I called Mrs. Brown. She said that she was in her nineties. She still went to church and drove a car sometimes. When I spoke to her, she seemed to have a sound mind. She told Sandy and me that she overheard her mother.

Mrs. Brown and other women in their gatherings said that my father's father was David Lucas. He was sneaking with her. (which meant having sex). So she was confident in what she heard about David Lucas being with my grandmother. Whether or not it was the truth, I did not have much doubt. I was still open to all information about my father's family.

Moreover, It felt good hearing Mrs. Brown said anything about anyone. I realized that it was a deposit to my empty spirit. After talking to Mrs. Brown for several weeks, I moved on to someone else whom Sandy found. This time a lady on my father's mother's side named Ruby Bass. She was my father's first cousin. I called Ruby Bass. She told me she had seen my father running around Florence, SC when she was very young. That was all she was able to say at the time. She also mentioned the Bass family, which was not close. There was a significant age difference between her mother and my grandmother. However, that was not the main reason for them not being close. It was just no one in the Bass family was close. I could only suspect it could be because my grandmother's father died at about age fifty-five in 1932. Times were hard. His wife died in 1928. My grandmother and some of her family moved to New Port News, VA. I was hearing that the family was not close to cousin Ruby. So it did not sit well with my spirit. Nevertheless, I tried to understand. She went on to tell me about her children and gave me her daughter's phone number.

I asked cousin Ruby if it was okay to call her back to talk with her in the future. She said okay. After a few weeks or so, I called cousin Ruby back. I got no answer several times. A few days later, my aunt Sandy said to me that cousin Ruby died. What little cousin Ruby said to me went a long way. It was the start of what was repeated by other Bass family members. I came across someone who said the same thing about the family. We were not close. This was an excellent deposit into my spirit. It also prepared one for what was to come. Not being close to family was sometimes a common theme of family falsehoods. Families get split where one side has nothing to do with the other. This means that family members do not fully benefit from another family member's experience.

I continued to talk to Sandy over the months and began to call her aunt Sandy affectionately. We got along well. Over time she shared everything she learned about her father and the Lucas family. I enjoyed and felt a deposit into my spirit. I also shared family documents with her that sometimes blew my mind. At this point, there was so much more to learn. Then I knew about my father's family. We had no DNA. So word of mouth and documents were all I had and a belief in finding the truth.

DEPOSITED DOCUMENTS

EARLY DOCUMENTS

1) Some of the early documents I acquired during my journey to find my father's family were his and my mother's marriage licenses. It said that he was from Florence, SC. I always thought he was from Portsmouth, VA, because he lived there when I visited him as a child. Another thing I took note of on the license because it stated his father's name, David Lucas.

Another document I had in my early research was my father's obituary. It stated that my father had a daughter, which would make her my sister. Her name was Felisa Taylor. I used that name to search for her early on to no avail. The obituary also stated that my father was a native of Florence, SC. His parents were David Lucas and Eva Bass. I also retrieved his social security application which also stated his father as David Lucas. On top of that, his first marriage certificate showed his father as David Lucas when he was married to my sister's mother, Felisa. After reading the information, I was convinced his father was David Lucas.

When I was in touch with Sandy Lucas, I always shared all my documents with her. But I came across something that was a big surprise. which made me a little confused.

Healthy Heart Diagram

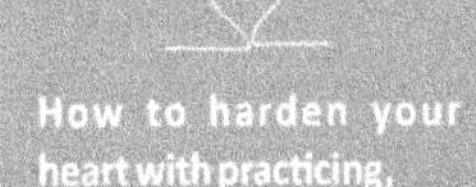

How to harden your heart with practicing,

- Hate, anger
- Arrogance
- self-centeredness
- Judgment
- Unforgiveness

How to tenderize your heart with practicing,

- Humility, openness
- love, caring
- service to others
- Spirituality, prayer Forgiveness

A unhealthy Heart is by our own willful and sinful choices. we can lose some ability to discern, we can lose sight of our direction in life. we can lose some wisdom.

A Healthy heart equals knowledge, understanding, compassion, and love flows through the heart like a blood flow. we gain sensitivity to the creators guidance and direction. we feel.

VISITED: WHERE MY FATHER WAS BORN, FLORENCE, SC.

I asked to see my father's birth certificate in South Carolina. The vital statistics office sent me a letter saying it had been sealed. They said the only way you could open it was to prove you were his son. Then we might send it to you. I sent what was requested to get the certificate. SO, it was mailed to me. When I received the birth certificate, I opened it. It said to my surprise that my father's name at birth was James Cantlo and his father's name was David Cantlo. It said the midwife was Maggie Brooks. I thought I was not related to Sandy Lucas. I was in disbelief. I called Sandy to share the news. I still wanted to believe that Sandy's family was my family. I said to her this was some coverup. The birth certificate was sealed to protect David Lucas. His mother could have done it because she was a midwife. I thought about it. I figured Maggie Brooks might be Maggie Lucas, David's mother, and David Cantlo might be David Lucas. I kept that possibility open in my mind to keep going. I could not stop here even though it had caused me some confusion. (My faith started to waver) (What a withdrawal of my spirit).

I felt more determined to get to the truth than before. So I committed to visiting my father's hometown. I made it a genealogy trip to see Sandy, Mrs. Brown, visit Pearl, and went to the town Clerk's Office to fish for records. I also wanted to go through my father's address where he once lived to see and absorb the feeling for a moment.

After talking it over with Sandy and others, I decided to visit Florence, SC, where my father and his family were from. I felt some motivation and willingness. I thought the trip would help me better understand my father. It might give me a sense of him growing up in the area. I talked to Al, a close buddy of mine, about going to South Carolina. I remember him speaking of his family. He went to visit them from time to time. He shared with me that he had a large family that was from Hemmingway, SC. He told me some of the stories to hope that I could have the same one day. It was almost like he spoke of ownership of something that I did not have. I felt that I was still looking for a deposit into an empty space.

My friend Al offered to take me to South Carolina to help me move since he was there and I had not. We left for South Carolina at two o'clock in the morning, traveling all night. In the morning, we checked into a hotel. Later that day, we started visiting, starting with Sandy. She was very friendly and helpful in assisting me in finding my family. We visited cousin Pearl. When I saw her, she was a short lady who was busy in the house. She hugged me and kiss. It made me feel welcome. Then, I met her husband and a few of her grandchildren.

We left cousin Pearl's house to go to Sandy's mother Ruby's house. I met Ruby and her son David Lucas Jr. with my friend there as my witness. I talked with them and looked at some pictures of Sandy's dad, David Lucas Sr, whom I suspected was my grandfather. As I looked at the images, I saw just a few similarities. Looking at Sandy's brother, I saw a little of him in myself, with the most significant difference being that he was short and tall. The most moving part of my visit to Sandy's mom's home was when she asked me to do her a favor. She did not look up to anybody else.

I listened with some understanding. However, I knew that I could not just stop there. I had one big fish to find, and that was my sister. The following person we visited was Mrs. Brown, who heard of my dad's father being Sandy's dad, David Lucas. Mrs. Brown was kind and very curious. When I first came through the door, she shouted, "you look just like your father." When she said this to me, I felt it in my spirit. She helped me feel some belonging to the family. It felt like a big deposit into my heart.

Moreover, she told us stories of her relationship with the Lucas family. During the visit, we all went out to eat several times and enjoyed the meal. We also went to a place where one of my friends Leroy from Darlington, SC, told me to check out. The site was the Thunderbird Inn that had some soul food. It was an old place, but the food was good.

Our journey to South Carolina also involved something in which Al and I had a mutual interest. We both enjoyed the history of Egypt. I found a seminar at Columbia University that talked about Egypt's history and had pictures of a guided tour. It was fantastic. Still, I have some memorabilia that I brought back to remind me how it felt and what I learned. While I was in Florence, I wanted to take a hard look at any records about my father and his close family. So Al and I visited the Town Clerks Office. The people were accommodating there. I found a fascinating record of my grandmother Eva Bass. It was the marriage certificate of her to David Cantlo. The date showed it was right before my father was born. This was a bit of a withdrawal of my spirit because it added to the confusion. It also said that my grandmother might not know who the father was at the time. I visited the address where my father once lived. There was now a Krispy Kreme at that address. I even took a ride to Effingham, SC, where my father was born, and Sandys's father and family lived. Before we left to go back to Connecticut, we stopped in Hemmingway, SC. So Al could visit his aunt for a little while. They talked about their family, which I enjoyed.

When I left Sandy, she said to me in a firm voice to find my sister when you get back to Connecticut. I had already attempted to find my sister, but I ran out of time. So I gave up and changed course to settle on any of my father's family. It was a blessing in my desire to find Sandy. It was because she became a huge encouragement for me to get the motivation and willingness that I needed to get back on the journey to find my sister. Sandy and I were sure that she could light up the father thing or get pictures or clues if we found her. Also, her mom or any of her relatives on her mom's side might provide something enlightening. This sister was a big rock unturned. So I set out to find my sister with Sandy as a guide. She told me she had a friend who worked in the South Carolina vital records department. She got information from her on finding the family.

After being back home for a while, I kept in touch with Sandy. I could call her aunt Sandy which felt right. She called me one day with some sad news. She told me that Pearl and her husband were driving from South Carolina to New York City to take care of some business their. and had a car accident. They both passed away from the accident. I was sad about the news knowing how kind and sweet Pearl was to me. I cant say enough about pearl who cared and shared with me all that was deposited into my spirit. I was blessed by her. She once said to me that you are my cousin and that felt right for me at the time. the love that pearl showed me still has some impact on me today, because when i think about my talks with cousin pearl it comforts my soul. I prayed for her and her husband to rest in peace.

FINDING MY SISTER

I tried unsuccessfully in the past to find my sister Felisa whom I knew like Peaches. My mother and the other sister Patsy told me that I had done it. Nobody could make me see her. I tried writing letters to people with her name. I found on our father's obituary saying her name was Felisa Taylor. I used to get a mailing list with her name. Then I mailed many letters to the name Taylor or Lucas like I was fishing for her. I even used the phone book from different cities that I thought she could be living in. However, nothing came back as a response or drop of information leading to her.

In 2002 I started again to look for my sister. This time, I had the help of Sandy. I did not know whether she would make a difference or not. Nevertheless, I was willing to try.

I remember when I came back to Connecticut after I was in Florence, SC. I spoke to my aunt Sandy a few times. Each time she asked me whether I had found my sister or not. She was a little pushy but persistent in encouraging me to get busy. I told Sandy I had no idea what else to do about looking for my sister. Sandy consulted with a friend who worked at the Town Clerks' office in vital statistics. The lady told Sandy to tell me to write a letter to the social security administration. She also suggested that I was looking for help finding my sister.

The social security letter sounded like a good idea. I wrote the letter with my background history and what I knew about my sister. They told me that they did not know enough about my sister's mother or surname. After a bit of time passed, I visited the Connecticut database in Hartford. I was told they had all the information if they were from Connecticut or married here. I scheduled a day to visit the database. By this time, I had some knowledge about genealogy and how to do some research. The day I went into the database, I knew I could not get on the computer myself unless I were a member of the genealogical society or a genealogist. I knew that I would have to rely on the person behind the counter for all my help. Fortunately, some good help came from the lady behind the counter at the database.

She took what I had, although that was not much. Then she returned with the information that showed all the times. My sister was married and all the last names she had. She gave me her mother's full name and her current last name from her stepdad. Those were more than enough to resend a letter to social security. I sent this information to social security as per their request. I waited for some time. A response came back saying we found your sister. They would be contacting her to see if she would accept your request to contact you.

My sister allowed me to have her number. I called her. In our first conversation, I was very nervous. She asked me whether I was drinking, partying, or going to clubs or not. I responded by saying I did not do either. I was recovering because of my spiritual journey. After that, I asked her about our father, whom I had an interest in. The only big question I asked her was whether she met our father's dad? She said she had met someone who said he was his father.

Nevertheless, she did not believe he was. She was speaking of David Lucas. I had also seen David Lucas on my first visit to South Carolina when I was a child. He was in a wheelchair. We did not know what his name was at the time. She also confirmed that our father was addicted to drugs heavily and spent some time in jail. My mother also said the same thing. We talked a few times back and forth. She was also excited about the fact that I had two children, which made her aunt. We then scheduled a visit for just the two of us. I drove to her house one day, bringing everything I had accumulated to share with her. When we first met, we both noticed a huge physical difference. She was 5 feet, but I was 6 feet tall. We both had the same father on our birth certificates.

I sat down with her and talked about my life. She spoke of hers. I then showed her some of the pictures and documents accumulated from my search. She looked at the photos of some of the Lucas family I had found. She said she believed our father's dad was very fair-complected. She said this because she had seen our father a few times. He was light skin complection. I did not think much about it because I wanted to believe this was our family.

I respected her belief. We moved forward in trying to establish a relationship with one another. We then met each other's families. I was very interested in meeting her mom, who was married to my dad for a short time. I had my ears open to everything she wanted to say, good or bad. When I first spoke to her, I asked her what she thought about my father. She said he was a druggie. He was not responsible, but he was handsome. She said I looked like him in the eyes, nose, and lips in the center of my face. I took in all that she told me as a deposit. Later, I started to think of my sister's mother as my mother and her step-father as my father. They were very kind and loving towards my family and me. I welcomed all the love they showed me.

My sister and I went on with our relationship visiting each other and getting together on holidays. It had been beautiful. Still, we are in touch. I love her much. On the other hand, I could not get her to want to call aunt Sandy.

She might have felt like there was a wall with too little information. It might bother to see her, to persuade her that I found the Lucas family in hers. I spoke to Sandy on many occasions. She had expressed some disappointment that my sister did not want to talk with her. It was the same with Sandy's brother Davy Jr. She did not believe that I was a part of his family either. That was what we both had to deal with moving forward. If my sister and I allowed our difference of opinions to get in the way, we would not move forward.

With my aunt Sandy, I did not let others get in our unique relationship. Otherwise, we could not love and support each other in good spirit. I stayed open. I allowed others to deposit what I needed in my heart. Each of my relationships was very valuable to me. Especially my sisters, whom I knew were related. My sister gave me deposits to fill my void by telling me everything she knew about our father. We all came to the point of accepting where we were in our relationships. I believed it was God's will. Everything was as it should be. In 2003 we had no access to DNA matches, at least at affordable prices to narrow things down. Our relationships stood the test of time until DNA became available. So we could get a better perspective.

It is now 2021. I am glad my sister and I had had a relationship long enough to take part in getting a DNA test. It became available to everyone from Ancestry.com. It was finally here to assist in setting some straight and improve my search. I confirmed that I am a Lucas which I had confidence in.

I initially thought about a DNA test through a suggestion from Sandy's distant cousin on a Facebook post. He sent me a message saying to help me. He told me to take a DNA test. I knew very little about it, but I kept an open mind. You never know where your help can come from. As I was recovering, I still had to keep in mind the practice of spiritual principles such as honesty. When I was confronted with how I was related to the Lucas family, I had to be 100% honest. I said that I was sure because I had some documents. DNA testing was starting to become popular increasingly at the time, around 2014 or so. I heard it repeatedly after I was on the Facebook group page for Lucas's family members with Sandy and her daughter. People were asking one another if they would get a DNA test. Even though I was a part of the Lucas Facebook group, it did not mean I was accepted into the family by all. Some were skeptical about me being related because only a few had heard of my father.

A few of Sandy's cousins challenged me, asking me whom I was related to etc. My aunt Sandy had to respond for me on a Lucas family Facebook group in the chat in capital letters saying, "THAT'S MY NEPHEW." I was learning an early lesson on this journey of family research. The lesson was that if you find a new relative, there is no guarantee they will accept you into their family or life. When I used to think about it, some of the relatives I knew were tribal. It was their tribe and my tribe. We did not get together or talked to one another. That was reality. Above all, my mission had to stay with finding out who was my father's father. DNA became a tool to help me achieve this goal.

Nevertheless, I moved forward to take this DNA test because I believed I was a Lucas. I was confident that I would match Sandy's family DNA. I got an Ancestry account first without the DNA and built a family tree with my main focus on the Lucas family. I put what I knew on the tree. I knew all of what Sandy told me.

Moreover, I knew others who had similar Lucas people on their tree who shared people with me. My tree had grown to hundreds of people. I also acquired more documents which were very enlightening. It was my father's census record at four years old. My grandmother and her then-husband named David Lucas. They were living in Newport News, VA.

I was happy for this record because it showed my father's father being David Lucas. I was always under the impression that Sandy's father, David, was my father's father. Even though the census states, David Lucas was born in GA. However, Sandys's father was born in SC. I rationalized it, saying this could be an error or something. Even so, Sandys's great grandfather was from GA. So it was possible still. The census record was from 1930, where they lived in Newport News, VA. It was known that many Florence, SC natives relocated too. Even Sandys's mother lived there for a while. Overall, it did cast some doubt on what I wanted to believe.

I searched on ancestry and added to my Lucas tree without my DNA. I was always willing to help anyone to find their family to put on to put the tree. Most people I encountered on ancestry were ready to help me, even the people you least expect. For the second or third time, one of Sandy's cousins asked me how I was related to the Lucas family. I did not have a solid answer. So in one sense, she seemed to want to help me. There could be an evil motive to take me away from my nephew/aunt's relationship with my aunt Sandy. This tied me to the Lucas family. I had in the back of my mind that she might also want to hurt Sandy. If I did not have a solid foundation of recovery, I would have given up. At times things did not look good, but glory to be God!

I kept an open mind. I thought of my motives to stay available to all sources of help, even if I had.

Some suppression was needed for me to let the thing play out. I had to remember that God is in charge and always cared for me even amidst trouble. I got a growing sense that Sandy and her cousin were not on the best of terms from their past. However, I had nothing to do with it. I did my DNA test and was waiting when her cousin reached out to me lastly on ancestry. We talked about DNA. She said a few Lucas family members would be putting their DNA on a GED match, a DNA matching site. I had my DNA test results back and started searching on ancestry. I did not quite know what I was doing yet. I took time to understand the matching of DNA.

In my early search, I did not see any clear DNA matches that said Lucas's family. Many people who might be related to the Lucas family did not have the last name, Lucas. It took a hard look at seeing whom they related to trace it to the Lucas family. Sandy's cousin reached out to me. She said if I had my DNA on the ancestry, I could go to the GED match to make the connection between Sandys Lucas and me. She told me what to do. I was a bit excited to get my match with Sandy's family. I was very confident in my compatibility with them. SO I rushed to get on a GED match and put my DNA up there. After looking hard, I saw no names with whom she said were on there. I was very disappointed and confused.

All I knew was supposed to be a Lucas. Because I was blinded and depressed, I decided to call Sandy. I wanted to let her know because I always shared everything with her. That was the fault of the cousins of mines. They were trying to cause us harm. Then I thought I had to stand back. I felt the best thing for me, but it was better to get out the Lucas group page on Facebook. So, I froze my account until more would be revealed. When I got out of Facebook, Sandy and her cousin had a total war on Facebook. They were saying mean things to one another that might be happening. Still, I can remember the last thing I shared with Sandy. After telling her that I did not see any Lucas match, she replied not to let the Devil Devour me. I was sure that I would be wounded in the crossfire of the Facebook family quarrel. I believe that timing is everything. I channeled that feeble feeling of confusion and anger into further researching what Lucas's family was related to. The rejection I felt from some of Sandy's cousins in the Lucas clan was a blessing in disguise. It was because it kept me motivated to look in other places for my father's family. My constant DNA search was all about the match I had seen related to a Lucas. I did this for months until my perception started to revolve around whether I had not gotten the right match to reveal something to me. That was a clear path to a Lucas family.

I then switched gears to looking elsewhere to find some clues on my DNA matches. I signed up at a family tree and up-loaded my DNA there. I went all in just searching matches on ancestry, GED, and family tree. I learned that I could put other family members' DNA on my ancestry account to help search. After looking on the family tree for Lucas's mother, there were little to no results. Then I sent them an email asking them that there might be an error in my DNA test. They responded and said No. I got a suggestion from someone to join a group project on the family tree. A group of people was only related to Lucas's family. However, you would need a Y DNA test. So I thought it was an excellent idea considering all else. It had not been enough to help me to see things clearly with my father's father's dilemma. I did the Y DNA and joined the Lucas group. The result was that I did not match any Lucas from all over the world. It was pretty shocking to find this out. I then asked the project administrator some questions. He said if your DNA was put in the group that says unrelated, then you might not be related to any Lucas but some other name.

With my disappointment and fire for the truth, I turned my attention to the DNA I could obtain to help my research. I knew it would be problematic in doing. Nevertheless, I felt I had to. I asked my sister, whom we had built a relationship with over the last 15 years, to let me had her DNA. She said yes with no hesitation. It took a while. The first test did not have enough samples to give a good result. However, the second one was good. After getting her DNA on my ancestry account, I was able to determine from our shared matches. If the two of us had a match, it would be on our father's side.

Then using DNA, I tried to leave no rock unturned. Since I was losing ground on finding a DNA match for the Lucas family, I started to turn away. My attention grew towards the Cantlo family. The name Cantlo came from David

Cantlo, who was on my father's sealed birth certificate and my grandmother's marriage certificate as her husband. I saw on the census that David Cantlo and his siblings lived next door to a Lucas family in Florence, SC. The lady who was the head of the home was named Mattie, which could have very well been Mattie Lucas.

This was a small town back in the 1920s and 1930s. I assume everybody knew each other. Many were related to each other. With this in mind, I stayed open to David Cantlo being a Lucas. I focused more on the ancestry of David Cantlo and could not find anyone to communicate with her. I had to go to my toolbox to find another solution for searching. I did a personnel search on one of the people's search websites that charged me a small fee. It worked. I was able to see the other women he had married. The Two sets of children had that were still living at the time. This was around 2017. After reaching out to the Cantlo folks, I found David Cantlo's youngest daughter in her forties. Her name was Denise. She was genuinely friendly and willing to help me.

Moreover, I explained that she could be related to me. It was because my father had her father's name on his birth certificate. My grandmother had been married to him. We exchanged information. She sent me a picture of her driving license.

Furthermore, she told me stories of him. She said she would ask a few relatives if they heard anything about her father's relationship with my grandmother Eva Bass. After she asked around, nothing came up.

I felt like there was nothing to lose if I asked Denise if she would do a DNA test for me. Let me knew the results. I would pay for it if she agreed to do it. Months went by. Nevertheless, I moved my attention to still searching for Lucas's family DNA matches to find anything as a clue. In 2017 some news came from my aunt Sandy. She told me that she was sick with cancer. She also said it was not good. I did whatever I could do to assure her that I would be there for you. I called her a little more. I came to visit her with my wife. She and her daughter visited me in the Atlanta area for a weekend. We had a good time. I took her to a festival where a couple of the Atlanta Housewives was. She was able to take pictures with Miss Bailey. When Sandy told my wife and me that she was a very good person, that was very heartfelt. I got Sandy to do a DNA test for me. I was very grateful. I started to see DNA as my best tool to sort out who was related to me and who was not.

This could bring me closer to who my father's father was. Afterward, I would know who that part of my family was. I filled my tree on my grandma's side, and I had many matches. I also met a few that I was related to, second and third cousins. Even though I made some connections to the Bass family, there were no solid relationships like

Sandy and me. I kept my foot on the peddle to find out the truth. It was in the middle somewhere. I reached out to Denise to see her DNA results because a few months had passed. I saw no matches on ancestry with her. She responded back and reluctantly told me that she did not match with me on ancestry. SO, she was a little disappointed and did not want to tell me. When I got this news from Denise, I shared it with my sister and Sandy. At this point, I ran out of leads or hope. I tried unsuccessfully to get Sandy's brother Davie to do a DNA test for me, including offering him $400. He said no before I had asked and gotten Sandy's DNA test sample. Davie also told me that he had done one before that a family member asked him to do. He was told that part of it was for my good, but no one told me his results.

Nevertheless, no one told me. I could have bypassed much research if I got Davies's DNA test results early on. However, in hindsight, I would have never met the people I had met along the way. Sometimes it is not good to arrive at your destination too soon or too fast. Especially if God's will is for you to fill yourselves with spirit as you would meet others. God sometimes needs to set you up for what is to come. So it becomes a significant and vital deposit into my spirit or heart. So by getting the information about DNA results with Denise, I could then pull the plug on the Cantlo family. It opened up a vast open space where I had no idea who my father was or his family. Only my faith could carry me forward at that time.

I got Sandy's DNA results back. It was a no match for my sister or me. I could see that she was related to Lucas's family ancestry. I shared this information with her and provided some copies of the cousin matches she had. This information was helpful to her in getting confirmation that, with DNA, she was a Lucas and belonged to the Lucas family of Effingham, SC. With no place to turn and find out who I was, I began to look for help. I initially sought to hire genealogical specialists. However, the cost was starting at $2,500.So, I thought hard about spending the money. I looked for less expensive options. One was to hire someone from a list at the Georgia Genealogy society. I did contact some, and they started at $500.

I then found a man named Ryan who had started a DNA analysis company called Missing Leaf. I contacted Ryan and told him what I was trying to do. He said I would charge you $250 if I could find out who your grandfather was. I would not charge you if I could not do that. I thought this was a good deal because what else did I have to lose. I allowed him to get started by managing my ancestry account to control my tree and DNA. During this same time, I felt I needed to look into any classes related to Genealogy. I found one right on time. The title of the course was "when you have hit the back wall." The title was fitting for how I felt defeated, powerless and confused. So all at the same time, I had a Missing Leaf looking at my DNA matches. I took the Y DNA at the family tree. Then I went to this class to get some help.

The class was a two-session class that was to meet Tuesdays and Thursdays. It also showed a willingness to find the truth. I traveled about two hours north in Georgia to a college to take this class. I had all these things going. I went to the class not knowing what I might hear. So I kept an open mind with my mouth shut. There were about 20 people in the class. Maybe half of them spoke about where they were in their search. Most of them stuck like me. After the class, I felt a little hope because I heard we might have to be patient. After all, things did not appear overnight in research. The next day I got on ancestry and searched a little. To my surprise, I found a death certificate that looked like it could clear up some things. It was the death certificate of David Lucas, of my father. It had on it Eva Bass as his wife, who was my grandmother. I eventually said I knew who my father's father was. The informant on the death certificate was a lady familiar with. I met her when I first visited with my father in Virginia. Her name was Emma Lawson. She used to be called Aunt Emma. My mother used to write letters to her to find out how my father was sometimes doing. Being excited about this document, I quickly put it on my Ancestry tree as my father's father.

I called Ryan from Missing Leaf to tell him of my magnificent find. I said, "Hey Ryan, I found him."

He answered, "No, it is not him or your family. You are not a Lucas. You are a Magruder." After he said that, I argued my point with the document I found. He answered back with the DNA matches that he found, which had a greater persuasion. He pointed out that I had a half-cousin, one-second cousin, and countless other third and fourth cousins. All related matches with the Magruder family. I was shocked at this time. I immediately went to my Ancestry account to verify this. Sure enough, I saw the matches.

Even though it was familiar, I was shocked that the matches were all European or white, but I was colored. I quickly gathered myself and started to process that my father was half white. No one in my life ever mentioned the name, Magruder. It just might be a family secret or just never brought up. According to his documents and whom he knew, it looked like my father settled in on his family, being the Lucas family. On Thursday, I returned to the class in north Georgia. This time I felt it would be time to share. It might be I could give someone some hope.

I talked about the things I discovered. The man running the class said, "yes, it sounds like you are a Magruder." When I left the class, a lovely lady came up to me before getting into my car. Then she spoke to me. The best thing I had heard from this lady had allowed me to look at things a little better. She said, "You were very focused on looking for the Lucas family because you wanted to believe." I saw she was right. When you want to believe in something, it is hard to let it go. At this point, I moved forward and continued to get confirmations every step of the way. One confirmation was I had my DNA test.

I looked at the general matches. Then I saw a Virginia Magruder as a third cousin. I signed up in Family Tree with a Magruder project using my Y DNA only for the father's line. When I was put on the Magruder project with all the matches from Magruder, it showed a solid match to me being a Magruder. All my father's forefathers were Magruders to Scotland. After a short time, I started to accept the fact that I am a Magruder. Through a Bass DNA match to a match with a Graham family member, I saw that they were strongly related to Emma Lawson and David Lucas.

I was curious as to how we were all connected. I reached out to the young lady on ancestry. She told me she was the great-granddaughter of Emma Lawson, the lady whom my father called aunt Emma. I then remembered that 30 years ago, I tried to call my mother's phone number for Emma Lawson to see if she had any information about my father's family or him. This time I was calling out the blue. My mother was deceased. So I had no one to ask anything about my father. When I called 30 years ago, I talked to Emma Lawson's granddaughter, the mother of this young lady I had connected with.

Realizing this, I asked her if I could speak to her mother. She said, "yes." I called Mrs. Graham. She told me that I was probably related to her husband on the Bass side of the family. She confirmed that Sandys's father was in the picture. Nevertheless, It was not like his father as a family. She also confirmed that David Lucas, her great uncle was not my father's biological father.

She said that my father was very, very fair-complected, which referred to him as almost white. I enlightened her with my new information about who her father could be, and she understood. She said that Sandys's father visited aunt Emma. Her brother David Lucas was seen as my father's adopted father. They called Sandy's father, young David Lucas, and the other the older David Lucas. I also got a document that confirmed their connection further. It was a military registration card of the older David, saying who his relative was. He mentioned on it that Henry Lucas was the name of David Lucas's father. He mentioned Henry as his uncle on his card.

DNA MAKES WAY

My search continued. However, I learned more about the Magruders and my grandfather named Thomas G Magruder Jr. I started to reach out to some of my Magruder matches first. I sent several messages through the Ancestry account to other members who had DNA matches with me. I got little to no response, mainly from 1st, 2nd, or 3rd cousins. I learned a lot about the DNA test and how to make connections through this process. I could triangulate the DNA matches around my grandfather. I thanked God. There were enough close cousin matches to see who he was. I also got some help in learning how my grandfather was similar to my dad and me. My sister was pointing out one by one, which was the long face of Thomas Magruder. My sister was more aware of our father's features because she visited him many times. The long face was even observed among other Magruders and my son. I believed it was a Magruder trait.

I began reaching out to the Magruder family on ancestry. The result was no response. I kept it going by reaching out to distant relatives to find out if anyone knew anything about Thomas G Magruder. Only a few responded. However, no one in their family knew him. I then shifted over to public information like Google. When I googled my grandfather's name Thomas Magruder Jr., much information came up about his career. He was a news reporter for the Washington Post. He had run several businesses, including a store with his then-wife in Williamsburg, VA. They sold imported clothing from Scotland.

I had seen that Thomas Jr. was married three times. I found out that he was a part of several organizations in his life. This might have something to do with his heritage. He seemed to be proud of his Scotland roots on his father's side and the name Magruder, which comes from Scotland. I deposited many things about Thomas into myself and my spirit. Some of them I still can identify with, like having a business. My son and daughter both have side businesses. I can also identify myself in wanting to learn more about your origins.

Interestingly, Thomas had put a family tree online years ago. It was public knowledge of his forefathers going back to Scotland. He had a similar desire as I had. The Crazy thing was he wanted to believe he was a Mcgregor. Later we found out he was not a Mcgregor because of DNA. It was proven, but he did not live long enough to see the proof. I also had the same experience believing that I was a Lucas. It was only to find out I was a Magruder through DNA proof only. Now, I live in this time of advanced genealogy research. Now I am searching for a natural person who can tell me anything good or bad about him. However, I found out about Thomas with some documents which are public knowledge. After reaching out to Magruder DNA matches on ancestry, I switched over to reaching out through Facebook. I knew the names of about ten or more Magruder-related people. I sent friend requests, but absolutely nothing came back as accepting. I waited some time, then tried again.

Nevertheless, no one responded. I then looked into some of the family I had close DNA matches with. I sent a friend request to some of them, but nothing was returned. I then went a little further and sent a friend request to anyone unknown. Then I was accepted. Acceptance was the moral of my story. I was trying to accept myself in this process better. I got a friend request received on Facebook.

I then asked two people if they knew my second cousin on the Magruder side of my DNA match. Then they said that they did. I asked them if they would reach out to them for me. Suppose they would be willing to talk to me or give me information about Thomas Magruder or his family. One person asked the 2nd cousin who worked with her what I said. The cousin responded quickly that they were friendly, that was all. I could only assume that she did not want to be bothered. Yes, she always had that right. I also felt I had the privilege to keep searching and asking someone else. It might be with a bit of faith in God. He would bring more light on Thomas Jr's life from someone else's perspective. I then bought a people search subscription to seek addresses and emails to reach out to others in this way. I sent emails to my close DNA matches.

Nevertheless, I did not get a response as I expected. Finally, I did get a response later. There had to be some communication about me in their family. It was because the cousin whose ancestors corresponded to the DNA finally sent me a message as if the family had convinced her to do so. I told them I was only looking for information about Thomas Magruder. For example, anything, such as smoking, drinking, etc., and what kind of cancer he had. I found this online, knowing that I only wanted to hear these things. I did not ask could I come over and be a part of your life. The message was sent to me in my Ancestry.com account.

She said in the message that Thomas Jr. was her grandfather on her mother's side, which she knew. She also said that he was not a very lovely person. He drank and was a significant player, meaning womanizer. He was a first-class bigot. His first wife, her grandmother, left him, and she also took her three children with her. She gave me an answer to my direct question, which she said Thomas died of lung cancer. He lived to be 80. I also saw that his son Dr. Thomas Magruder the third, died around the same age, 80. She ended by saying she had no intention of reaching our family tree. Which said to me she did not want anything to do with any of his family. So I believed that this also included me. With this information, I was some things needed to be looked at beneath the surface. Thomas seems to have symptoms of a person acting out like my father. I also used to be the same when we were in active addiction. I could assume that I got the disease of addiction from my father and his father. It was not clear. However, the most important thing was that I had a new lifestyle. Which means that I did not chase women or smoke or drink. Now, I view all that my DNA match person provided positive input into my mind and heart. I have love and compassion for all families who have pain and suffering at the hands of another family. There is hope and healing for all that we seek. This is a deposit that helped to fill and keep filling my void. Influence is a strong word. I am using it to decrease what I felt from people who became important to me and my spirit.

LUCAS, MAGRUDER FAMILY SEARCH

My most noteworthy influence in this search was to fill a father's void. Aunt Sandy Lucas almost had the same relationship with me as my father's with his aunt Emma Lawson. Aunt Sandy was not my biological aunt, but it felt as if she was. Just like my father's aunt Emma, she was not his biological aunt. Nevertheless, she behaved as if she was. The main thing we both got was help from our aunts. How miraculous to have such a person in our life. Unfortunately, my aunt Sandy passed away on the 27th of August 2018. She had battled against cancer for about a year. I was able to give her moral support in her time of struggle. I used to go to her home service and bought some flowers. It was like the plug being pulled for the whole Lucas family in my life. I only really knew her, but she knew many Lucas family members. It was as if I knew them, too. It was because I had a solid bond with her for 17 years. Still today, I am grateful for the experience with aunt Sandy. It truly helped my father void as we both bought my and her father to life spiritually.

When I was a child, I first became aware of a need and desire for a father. My mother's boyfriend was there for me as a father figure. I had no idea what had gone on between my mother and the biological father, so that they had to separate. I knew I had something in myself that wanted that paternal love. My mother's boyfriend became my immediate replacement for filing my need. However, it was not the best. My mother's boyfriend Charles was only over at our house on the weekend sometimes. I remember crying when he was supposed to go. I also remember when he came to stay, my mom put him out for whatever reason.

Over time my relationship with Charles Wiley grew. My mother started to allow him to buy me things and discipline me as well. When I was about eight or nine, my mother married Charles. He became my full-time father with all the ups and downs. We did not spend much time together. Throughout our time together as father-son, the main focus became, take out the trash, clean up your room, get in the house, eat your food. Lastly, get my belt house for going to beat your butt. My step-father knew what he was taught when he was a child. However, he was also limited in his parent package because his mother died when he was a kid. His father raised him most of his life.

The way he raised me was like disciplinary, where you were punished for every wrong but not much talking. I did have a few fun things that I can still remember. Those were like showing me how to build model ships with glue. I also went to work with him on a few occasions to take out the trash, full of a few orders etc. After a few years as a step-father, I noticed that he went further in his alcohol addiction. My mother said that he started to change after coming back from Germany when he visited his daughter for the first time. I believed this was a big thing for him. However, whatever his internal environment was, it seemed to be showing itself in the bottle. After a few years, my step-father's alcoholism had become full-blown, which affected me and everyone. Mainly it affected my mother's relationship with him. He lost his job. Then he got divorced from my mother. What seemed to be a perfect replacement for the father became an additional emptiness in my life. When I was 23, he was gone, just like my mother. My mother also had passed away when I was 23 years old. So at this stage of my life, I was low and willing to get any help that I could get.

After a few months, my step-father called me to come to where he lived. At the time, he was living in a rundown rooming house. I spoke to him. He told me how I would feel if he came over and rented me a room and helped me into the house. This was almost like a deal or agreement. So I thought about it a day or so and said, "yes." Over time this becomes more of a friendship than a father-son relationship. This was also an opportunity for us to get to a better place than in the past. He still drank but not as heavy as he used to. As time went on, he witnessed me getting married and having children, living life. He became my encourager and friend. He witnessed me going through my tough times of addiction. We grew together in many ways as adults. This growing relationship was different. It made a small deposit into my spirit, especially when I lost the home we were living in due to my addiction. When we lived apart, we were locked into mutual aid. The relationship got better again when I got myself together in 1994. I could be there more for him. It allowed my void to get filled even more. Later, perhaps five years later, my father stopped drinking and smoking at about 65. His doctor said he would live about ten years more if he did.

I remember him about to give up drinking. He asked me how it was not to use anything. I told him what I did and was essential to sustaining recovery: a closer relationship with God. I came to understand. I said that I prayed and did spiritual things that helped my spirituality. He stopped drinking. As a result, his health got better, as his doctor said. We gelled better than before. Our conversations were better, and most things were better with us. For the next ten years, my step-father and I were good friends. We supported one another the best way we could. When I needed the truth about my biological father, he gave me what he knew. He told me that he would help my mother from time to time to get my biological father out of the drug house to bring him home.

He had witnessed how miserable my father was. It was the main reason my biological father and mother split. When my step-father's health began to fail, he came to me. He asked that I took care of his affairs if something terrible happened to him. I felt honored that he cared so deeply for me and trusted me. I said, "yes." I would do whatever you would need me to do. He had one special request. It was to compensate some of his insurance money. When he passed, I did exactly what he asked me to do. It feels good to do it lovingly. When he died, it was a loss for me but a win for us on our journey to seal the deal.

DIRECT FATHERLY REPLACEMENTS REMEMBERED

GOD FATHERING

When I was about 12, I met a guy named Chris that just moved around the corner from me. We liked each other's company. So we formed a friendship, going to each other's houses and hanging out. I loved going to his house more and more because I had an attraction to his whole family life. It was nothing like mine. They were elegant and organized.

Moreover, they went places together. They started to take me with them. I started to love being at their house. I later wished I could live with them. During this time, my step-father was going downhill with his alcoholism. Eventually, he lost his excellent job. That caused several other problems in my household. I always look back to see how influential my friend's father was in my life. He took a little time with me to teach me some things like carpentry and fixing things. I loved how he had many tools in his basement and garage and was meticulously organized. I think he liked me because I always had more interest than his two sons in fixing things. Over time, I paid attention to my friend's father's life. He became the father I would love to have.

I was truly fortunate to go places with my friend and his father. Like on Sundays, we went to the flea market where he would look for tools to buy early in the morning. He was getting me a hot chocolate, which I liked. He let me worked on some things in his workshop a few times, like making a pair of stereo speakers. My friend would be rushing me to finish to go outside and play. I observed many things about my friend's father. Mostly the many ways he took care of his family. He was also very protective. I even got some driving training in his driveway. He would sometimes ask me to pull the car up to the garage. Many of the things he told me strengthened my self-esteem. He once told me that I was a good friend because I would assist with garden work, etc. He was helping me understand friendship as a two-way street. I help you, and you help me. When I was 16, they adopted me as godfather and godchild. They are my extended family still today. It was a blessing for me to be a part of my friend's family.

I needed to be around a good family who might help me one day. I leaned on my godfather and his family through my mother and step-father's divorce. AT that time, I was about 16 in the early 1970s. My godfathers' influence was significant in my development of what a good father should look like. Alternatively, how I would like to be if I were a father. Since I became a father, I had consulted my godfather to ask him about his opinion on things on many occasions. He always gave me honest, straightforward, simple advice. Still, I hold on to what he said. He always concluded by just saying do the right thing. When I got older and sometimes struggled to afford to take my car to the shop for repair, I would ask my godfather to use his tools and garage to fix my car.

He would always say yes as long as I followed his rules in the process. Those were like cleaning up afterward and putting back the tools I used where I got them from. When I came to fix or repair something that belonged to me, I always received more than I wanted by being with him and talking to him. Many of my memories of interacting with my godfather made me feel grateful that he was in my life. As a result of getting help from him as I was growing up, I tried to give him back if he needed me. Over the years, I have had the opportunity to thank him by helping him at home and visiting him. My godfather is in his 80's now. I am glad that he has lived so long and had a great life. I have seen him help many people. It demonstrates that he has a good heart.

Being a father, I have incorporated some of my godfather's ways and means in my life. I always wanted to have a garage with tools. I try to keep it neat. I do have a garage with tools but nothing like my godfathers. I try to be the man of the house and act like it. When any problem arises in my home, I try to step up and take care of it. I have always tried to be a good provider for my family. I watched my godfather did those well. The way I become a father came from a group of people.

Nevertheless, my godfather was the best model I had early on in my beginnings as a father. I also use spiritual principles. My own experience as a father helps bridge my void.

Without my efforts to change years ago, my children might have been subject to my abandonment. Then the intergenerational trauma would continue. When my kids were 8 and 10, I became more present in their lives. I was always there physically. I started to participate more in their lives. We went on vacation, and I rode the amusement rides with them. We went on holiday regularly. As a result of maintaining a presence in my son's life, he was better in his last stage of growth and development. That means they would transition from boyhood to manhood well.

When my son played sports, I made an effort to be his biggest fan and be in place. I got some words of wisdom from a parent who raised their sons well. I asked him how he did it. He said that I showed up for my kids no matter what they did. I confirmed what I felt I was already doing. I then saw the fruits of my labor when my kids got through high school successfully. They also had good grades. Then they went to college and had the same success. They went on to be independent and live a life for themselves that they want. I am enormously proud of them. At this point, I may have escaped being a father void.

Nevertheless, I am sure I was sometimes him roid. In other words, a pain in their butt. It is important to note that growing up without a father could permanently alter the brain's structure.

When it comes to being a father, I wish I were the father I wanted. Over time I have realized that when I am doing well in my life, being in good health, mentally and spiritually, then I will be at my best as a father. That has been my experience. I have been a good father to my two children, especially over the last 27 years. Still, I am their father but in a different way. Now they are all grown up and living their own separate lives. It still fills my mind when I am asked to advise my children as a father. The void today must still be filled. It happens in many of God's ways. All I have to do is stay prepared and open to whatever God sends or puts in my way. We keep what we have by giving it away. What was freely given to me was God's father's influence.

I had other influences in my life that were not in direct contact with me. Nevertheless, I heard of them from my mother. My mother always spoke highly of her uncle Mack who stepped into her life. It was when her father died, and she was a little girl. Even though uncle Mack had many children, he was available for my mother, making her forever grateful. I only knew about being an uncle through my mother's view of how she spoke highly of her uncle Mack. Later, I became an uncle like Uncle Mack because my sister passed away at 47 and was 36.

I stepped up for my nephews and nieces to be there for them whenever I could do. Yet today, they looked at me for what I did for them. This was another opportunity to serve God in the process of filling my father void by being a father like to others. It was because they did not have their fathers in their life. They told me that the highest aspiration of the human heart was to help somebody. It was something God has entrusted with us we serve.

Suppose you have had fatherlessness in your life that has caused you to spiritually limp. Your solution may be to get a spiritual one so that it can help you walk through life. That can come in the form of forgiveness of yourself or others. Love is the message here. More self-love can help you love others. Others may not get better, but you can. Try to do something that speaks to your healing. Pray, join a positive organization and volunteer, try therapy. Contact your father's family to find out more about him and his immediate family. You may find out more about yourself by seeing similar traits. The apple does not fall far off the tree. Give yourself a break, and break what is in the way of your growth.

Overall, from generation to generation, there is always hope, no matter what your pain, trauma, or hopelessness may be. Although our pains may be different, our recovery or treatment is also different. Our goal is to feel, deal with, and heal.

To achieve some relief, live better in peace and harmony with self and others, and ultimately have peace with God. Blessed are those who get to the other side of their pain. Too much pain from anyone becomes a pain in the behind or butt. Too much pain for too long can become like him roid. Also, it can become more than just a pain in the butt, but a pain in your spirit, Psyche. Then possibly, it causes a limp in your walk-through life.

My father was in pursuit. I was finding and reaching his goals in life of being a good man, having healthy relationships with self and others, reaching a place of balance. However, he was stopped short of his goals by some of his unresolved issues when he medicated with drugs, women, and alcohol. He had gone in that direction for so long without addressing the problem. Moreover, he developed a using mentality. There was some indication that his best treatment for his recovery was not maintained. It was spiritual counseling for his pain and trauma. My mother once said that my father was at his best when he read Bible.

My step-father was stopped short of his goal of having a happy family life. Moreover, enjoying all the blessings, he had an excellent job, home, wife, a beautiful German shepherd. Nevertheless, it all came to a halt as his alcoholism started to progress.

Over time the more my step-father used alcohol, the more painful it became. Moreover, the more pain he inflicted on the closest people around him, like my mother and his coworkers. Over time I watched him lose his wife, job and put pressure on, jeopardizing his health. I watched him be encouraged by his doctor late in his life when he was around 65. He (Doctor) had told him to let go of the alcohol and cigarettes for good for many years. Then you might add another ten years to your life. He did just that and lived another ten years, passing away at 75. During these ten years of his life, he and I had the best relationship we had ever had. His health also improved. Our relationship blossomed like a flower. Part of his treatment was prayer, reading the word, and helping others. When he was in denial about his drinking, I watched him go to the hospital to dry up. They called it, was not drinking for two weeks. When he came back from his dry out, he would say, I was okay because I went two weeks without a drink.

Nevertheless, he would go right back to where he left off, heading back downhill. During the worse days of his drinking, even the dog ran from him when he got drunk.

Thank God we survived. Nevertheless, it was not without a few emotional scars.

As for me, I had goals in life that could not be realized because of some effects of my parents on me and what I put myself. In my late teens, I started college and wanted to become a CPA. Nevertheless, I could not reach that goal because I smoked marijuana. I was wrong because I thought it was making me think better. After moving past all my father's issues, I became an enrolled agent, close to being a CPA. The goal of many parents consciously or subconsciously was obedience and control. So, I lacked some of the discipline needed, especially in my early childhood being fatherless. My mother was taking on this role of father. She was sometimes very passive, allowing me to get away with this most of the time. Then my mother's boyfriend married her and became my stepfather. Then I was 8 or 9 years old. He was overly obedient, controlling me. My mother stood back and let him do as he pleased. The reason my stepfather was like this was that his father was highly disciplinary.

Nevertheless, after a few years, things turned in a more negative direction. My stepfather went to Germany to visit his daughter for the first time. She was a grown woman at that time. At this time, his problems just got started. At first glance, his alcohol consumption increased until it became an issue for him and his family. At 12 or so, his disciplining me started to fade as I started to rebel with balling up my fist with anger. So, the effects of alcoholism on me started to fit the literature about where trauma comes from fatherlessness. Father void formed having a father, but it was not good having a father when they were not stable. It was said that fatherlessness could cause you to have psychological effects and be prone to low self-esteem. More likely to be depressed, be more aggressive, do poorly in school, use drugs, and have control issues. I am sure I can say that I have experienced most of this at some point in my life. Truthfully, I was not aware that I was negatively affected by my fatherlessness throughout my adult life.

My sister, with whom we shared the same father, was abandoned by him like me after six months. It had negatively affected her too. The anger poison she got from our father caused her many failed male relationships. A possible intergenerational problem could have been when I took off with drug abuse as a young teenager at 13. My reaction to drugs was the same as my biological father's. One was too many, and one hundred was never sufficient. It is important to note that my drug use contributed to missing a step in my last growth and development stage of life. The fact that I had a stepfather.

Nevertheless, he was not emotionally present enough to help me transition from boy to man. It was a critical stage for any young man. In the beginning, it felt good using drugs. I did not know how much I was medicating. Some bad feelings I had inside, which I never got a chance to talk about. At the age of 36, once I got rid of all the drugs that changed my spirit and mood, I was able to see things more clearly about myself. Then I picked up the pieces that felt off along my path of self-destruction. In recovery at 36, I started to recover myself as a parent. I worked to be a better father to my two children when they were 8 and 10 years old. I worked alongside my wife in parenting, like being a team player. I did not have a double parent.

If parents are not on the same team, they open the door for children to split the parents. Meaning when they do not get what they want, they go to the other. I discovered that we were better together on one side than doing something different when there were problems and issues with children. Later, my goal became to be the father I would have loved to have. I have achieved that goal because I feel good about being a father. Now I am a grandfather. My children also claim that I am a good father, which is external confirmation. I am blessed to have all the opportunities to recover myself as a person and father. I also improve my attitudes about my fathers in my life. I try to maintain all that I have gained by practicing increased love and forgiveness. I always gain a better perspective when looking at myself. My imperfections were of being fully human. My principal teacher was always the one on whom I learned to support myself through my life lessons. He was godfather. I maintain my sanity with spiritual therapy mixed with prayer daily.

Always remember to seek help if you feel you have a father issue. One kind of treatment may not be suitable for everyone. Find the treatment that works for you but do not forget to look at yourself in the process. Recovery begins and ends with you.

Fathers do not just simply walk away from their family and abandon their children because of laziness or lack of love. They may leave for many other reasons; they may leave because they feel unworthy. Some reasons for feeling unworthy are personal problems unrecognized like addiction, alcoholism, or traumas etc. This can give a father a false sense of parenting not knowing the impact that some of their unresolved personal problems will set them up for failure for, when attempting to be a successful father. So, when becoming a father, it is important to take your own inventory to find out what you need to do to be as all around healthy as you can be to help your child grow up with as much love and affection needed for their successful growth and development to adulthood.

There is a father absence crisis in America.

According to the U.S. Census Bureau, 18.3 million children (about the population of New York), 1 in 4, live without a biological, step, or adoptive father in the home. Consequently, there is a father factor in nearly all social **ills facing America today.** Source: U.S. Census Bureau. (2020). Living arrangements of children under 18 years old: 1960 to present. Washington, D.C.: U.S. Census Bureau.

www.ingramcontent.com/pod-product-compliance
Lightning Source LLC
Chambersburg PA
CBHW032121280326
41933CB00009B/943

9780578976938